Taking Authority Over Your Circumstances

Dr. RONNIE L. MCCRAY

Taking Authority Over Your Circumstances

Dr. RONNIE L. MCCRAY

NVP
NUVISION PUBLISHING

ISBN: 978-0-578-64611-4 (Paperback)

NUVISION PUBLISHING

Published by
NuVision Publishing
PO Box 4455
Wilmington NC 28406
www.nuvisiondesigns.biz/publications

Printed in the United States of America.

FOREWORD

I have been blessed to directly receive the teachings in this book, Taking Authority Over Your Circumstances. Without a shadow of a doubt it is an effective tool that will help you master life's challenges. Based on biblical principles, the application of speaking God's creative word is fail proof.

We may be familiar with the idea of reciting affirmations and/or voicing our dreams, however, speaking words designed to bring things into existence guarantees the correct outcome. The purpose of God's Word is to have the power to accomplish what is spoken. His Word will manifest. Our role is to speak the Word in faith believing what we speak to be true. Affirmations help increase our faith and expectation level; the

Word of God is obligated to do whatsoever we ask. What an eye-opening revelation! If we become familiar with His Word, training ourselves to use (quote) the Word, what we speak in faith shall be done. This is the Father's law which cannot be changed, written for our benefit so we can Take Authority Over Our Circumstances.

Corrine E. McCray, CLC
Gracefully Led Life & Spiritual Coaching

TABLE OF CONTENTS

INTRODUCTION

Millions of people today are struggling with life's circumstances. Too many of us are unaware that we have been granted authority by God. We often do not realize the authority we have been given by the Lord Jesus Christ. This book will teach you how to recognize and take authority over any situation that comes your way.

The purpose of this book is to help you navigate through life's journey with a smile on your face, knowing you are more than a conqueror through Christ Jesus. This book will inspire, encourage, and bring you to the awareness that you can take authority over your circumstances. I am delighted to write this book to help open your spiritual eyes. Once the spiritual eyes are open, you will begin to see life in a different way. The Lord put this book in my heart many years ago when I was praying about a situation, he said to me, "I have given you authority over your circumstances, now take authority over your circumstances and not allow your circumstance to take authority over you." May you be richly blessed by this text.

Chapter One

Taking Authority Over Your Circumstances

Authority is defined as the power or right to give orders, make decisions and enforce obedience. Human existence is not without authority, as it is through this platform, balance is maintained. For example, a law enforcement officer has been delegated the authority to enforce obedience, in that, he is charged with the power to enforce or administer the law. The Bible lets us know, all authority and power was given unto the Lord Jesus Christ, and He has delegated that authority to us. Let's look at the 1st chapter of Genesis, verses 26-28: ***"And God said, let us make man in our image, after our likeness: and let them have dominion over the fish of the sea, and over the fowl of the air, and over the cattle, and over all the earth, and*** *over every creeping thing that creeps upon the earth. So God created man in His own image, in the image of God created He him; male and female created He them. And God blessed them, and God said unto them, Be fruitful, and multiply, and replenish the earth, and subdue it: and have dominion over the fish of the sea, and over the fowl of the air, and over every living thing that moves upon the earth."*

We see here, that in the beginning, man was created in the image of God. The word image speaks of reflection or likeness, which has to do with character. Character must be developed through due process. It has a series of actions accompanied by desired outcomes. The word dominion means to have rulership or to manage. Notice that God gave dominion (willfully) to them; both male and female.

In verse 28, He charged them 'to be fruitful and multiply' and gave them authority and dominion over *'the fish of the sea, the fowls of the air, and every living thing that moves upon the earth'.* God did not give man authority over man, but He gave them authority and dominion over creatures that exist in all dimensions, upon the earth. We must understand that, from the beginning, God gave them - male and female - authority. In other words, they were both charged with the power to enforce, to make decisions and to give orders. The principle about authority, however, is that when we do not use our authority, we will lose it.

In Genesis chapter two verse seven, we find the account of how man was created: *"And the Lord God formed man of the dust of the ground, and breathed into his nostrils the breath of life,*

and man became a living soul".

Man is a spirit; he has a soul and lives in a body. In Genesis, the first chapter (verse 26) God created man, and in Genesis, the second chapter (verse 7) we find that God formed man of the dust of the ground. He then breathed into man's nostrils the breath of life. Man came to be, not to do. The bible does not inform us that he tried to be a man. Man was mature and full grown from creation. When God breathed His spirit into the formed body, man became a living soul, living inside of an earthly body. Man did not come to do; man came to be. The first man, called Adam, did not have to try to be a man, he was a man. The Bible also declares man is God's masterpiece and He has delegated His authority to mankind to operate in the earth realm (Genesis 1:27-28).

Let us look at the word 'circumstance' which

is derived from the Latin word circumstare or 'circle'. A circle is a round plane figure whose boundary (the circumference) consists of points equidistant from a fixed point (the center). As long as you are in a circle, box, or comfort zone, you limit what God can do for you. When we learn how to come out of our circle (circumstances), we open the doors to the supernatural where all things are possible to those that believe. In doing this, we take the limits off ourselves and what God can do for us, and through us.

Daily we deal with circumstances and situations. I know sometimes it's hard to come out of something we are used to. But we do not have to let our circumstances take authority over our lives. Our circumstance is something we create in our minds. We can change our circumstances by adjusting our mindsets. Stop allowing your circumstances to take authority over you.

There are two things that God will not do. *Firstly,* God will not intervene in your will. *Secondly*, God will not go against His word. God has given man free will to choose. Free will is a gift from God. We learn in Genesis, that Adam and Eve were instructed not to eat from the tree of knowledge of good and evil (Genesis 2:17). Despite this, they gave in to their free will and acted contrary to God's request. When they disobeyed (sinned against) God, they lost their authority and the ability to connect with their spirit. Whenever we sin, it disconnects us from the source, which is our spirit. Whenever you are disconnected from the spirit, you are operating in your flesh, thereby giving your flesh authority over your spirit. Your spirit is meant to rule over your flesh. When we operate in our flesh, we will fulfill the lust of the flesh. But if we walk in the spirit, we will fulfill the things of the spirit. Our flesh (bodies) houses the soul and spirit. The Bible teaches us that there is nothing good in the flesh (Romans 7:18). The flesh daily wars with the spirit. Having full knowledge of the authority and power within us, helps us to keep the flesh subdued so we do not become victims to our circumstances.

As children of God who are walking in authority, when we get trapped in our circumstances, God always makes a way for our escape. The 10th chapter of First Corinthians, verse 13 states: ***"There hath no temptation taken you but such as is common to man: but God is faithful, who will not suffer you to be tempted above that ye are able; but will with the temptation also make a way to escape, that ye may be able to bear it."***

God will not put more on you than you can bear. When we yield ourselves to Him, God will always bring us out (and on top of) our circumstances. The Apostle Paul reminds us, in the book of First Corinthians, that through our relationship with Christ, we can have dominion over our circumstances. Paul writes, ***"I can do all things through Christ which strengthens me"*** (Philippians 4:13). The context of this verse focuses on the God-given power to endure any circumstance that may come our way. When we come to the realization that we have inherited divine authority in the name of Jesus, and start using that authority, our lives change.

So, we must develop the correct propensity to come out of our negative circumstances. Come out of your comfort zone. Come out of your little box. Activate the power that God has already given you and start walking in the supernatural power of Christ where all things are possible to those who believe. Do you not know that you create your own circumstances by what you believe to be 'truth'? Too many times, believers in the church accept their challenges and circumstances without exercising authority. They give power (and many times give in) to their circumstances without even realizing it. Hence, the circumstances seem never-ending.

However, every circumstance can be changed. First, we must change the way we think. Yes, our thinking mechanism must be significantly re-wired. If we do the same thing over and over again, we will only get the same results. If we want to change our results, we must change our thinking. When we think negative, we attract negativity to us. When we think positively, we attract positivity

19

to us. The Bible states, ***"Finally, brethren, whatsoever things are true, whatsoever things are honest, whatsoever things are just, whatsoever things are pure, whatsoever things are lovely, whatsoever things are of a good report; if there be any virtue, and if there be any praise, think on these things"*** (Philippians 4:8). Your thoughts help to create your experiences. Whenever you process a thought and act on it, it then becomes your experience. In other words, it becomes your reality. Remember we are spirits - speaking beings - having an earthly experience. We create our experience by processing thoughts and speaking words. Whatever you see in the spirit realm, you can bring it into the natural realm, once we begin to take authority in what we speak. All things are possible to them that believe.

Chapter Two

Faith In Action

By nature, mankind believes with the heart, and we also believe words. The book of St. Mark tells us how belief and words intertwine. In St. Mark 11:22 the scripture says: ***"And Jesus answering said unto them, have faith in God."*** What the writer deposits in our spirit here, is that we should have the "God kind of faith". When we have the God kind of faith, we can do everything that God said we can do. A closer examination of verse 2 reveals even more: ***"For verily I say unto you that whosoever shall say unto this mountain, be thou removed and be thou cast into the sea and shall not doubt in his heart, but shall believe that those things which he says shall come to pass, he shall have whatsoever he said."*** Notice what Jesus said, 'Whosoever shall say unto this mountain.' We must, first of all, speak to our mountains or circumstances. Nothing will change until we speak to these circumstances. A mountain can be any situation in your life that looks big or impossible. If we say to the mountain 'be thou removed', the mountain must be removed because words are very powerful. When you speak in faith, it will move. Only in faith believing can you activate the word of God over your circumstances. When we speak the word of God over any situation, things will change. I said, things will change! This biblical principle will work for any one who has the faith. Faith without works is dead. Your speech is the work that will activate faith. Let's look at Mark 4:35-41: *"And the same day, when the evening was come, he said unto them, Let us pass over onto the other side. And when they had sent away*

24

the multitude, they took him even as he was in the ship. And there were also with him other little ships. And there arose a great storm of wind, and the waves beat into the ship, so that it was now full. And he was in the hinder part of the ship, asleep on a pillow: and they awake him, and say unto him, 'Master, carest thou not that we perish?' And he arose, and rebuked the wind, and said unto the sea, 'Peace, be still.' And the wind ceased, and there was a great calm. And he said unto them, 'Why are ye so fearful? How is it that ye have no faith?' And they feared exceedingly, and said one to another, 'What manner of man is this, that even the wind and the sea obey him?'"

Notice what Jesus said to his disciples, 'Let us pass over onto the other side'. Anytime Jesus asks us to do something, it will come with a challenge. The devil will try to put something in our path to stop us from doing what God has called us to do. It is time to go to the other side! It is time to step out of the box or circle that we have been trapped in for some time. It is time to step into the supernatural where all things are possible to those who believe. My question to you is, where did the storm come from? The storm could not have come from God. Jesus instructed the disciples to cross over. The Father and Son work together and are in agreement. So, this tells us that the storm came from the devil. His job is to try to stop you from going to the next dimension. He does not want you to break free out of your circumstances and get to the side where Jesus has something better for you. His desire is to keep you ensnared or trapped in your circumstances, but God is instructing you to 'go to the other side'.

When God gets ready to do something in your

life, sometimes He will isolate you from the multitude, because people can hinder you from going into your destiny. Jesus' charge to His disciples to 'go to the other side', is His indication that they have to act in order to be moved from their current circumstances or predicament.

As they began to cross over, all of a sudden, a storm came. We all have many different kinds of storms in our lives. Don't be afraid of the storms because storms come and go. The disciples, afraid of the storm, went down to the hinder part of the ship to wake Jesus. Notice how Jesus dealt with the situation. When Jesus arose, he rebuked the storm and said, "Peace, be still", and there was a great calm.

How did Jesus deal with the situation? He spoke to the problem and the problem went away. So then, we must learn to speak to our problems.

We should let our problems know how big our God is. The Bible tells us that *'God has not given us the spirit of fear, but of love and a sound mind'* (2nd Timothy 1:7). Fear is the opposite of faith. Faith and love casts out fear. Jesus said to his disciples, **"Why are you so fearful and how is it that ye have no faith"?** The disciples were amazed that the wind and the sea obeyed him. They said, *"What manner of man is this that even the wind and the sea obey him"?* If Jesus demonstrated His power in this fashion and equipped us with His Spirit to do the same, then you should tap into your power and activate your authority. Things will also obey you if you apply the word of God over your situation.

The Bible declares, in the book of Psalms, chapter 103 verse 20, *"The angels of the Lord will hearken unto the voice of God's word."* God's word becomes activated when you speak it. When we speak God's word in faith, the angels will obey as though God Himself has spoken. As believers, we have authority in the name of Jesus to profess God's word. Everything is subject to the word of God. Even time, space and matter must obey the voice of the Creator. In the beginning when God created this universe, He did so by His spoken word.

One of the things God created, was time. God himself has no time. He is outside of time. Time was not made to rule or to have authority over man, but man was created to rule over time. When Adam sinned, things were turned upside down. Instead of time serving man, man is now serving time. Time is an element like matter; you can't see it and it is temporary. We must understand that God does not exist in time because he is the author of time. He created time to serve us, and not for us to serve time. When we are born again through baptism, and through our acceptance of Jesus Christ as our Lord and Savior, we become free from the constraints of time. We are no longer functioning in time, but instead, we are functioning in faith.

Faith is a higher law than time. Faith tells time what to do. Faith is now! Time can be later, or tomorrow, but faith is NOW. We have the authority to bring our future into our now. Whatever you see in the spirit realm or through your eyes of faith, you can bring to you NOW. This is because faith goes into your future and brings your future to your NOW. You can be healed, NOW. You can be blessed, NOW. You can be set free, NOW. You can be happy, NOW. If you give your faith an assignment, it will work for you every time.

Everything God has done for you, He did it from the beginning. God always finishes a product, before He starts it. GOD FINISHES YOU, put you back in time, then starts you afresh. Everything has been finished from the beginning. Everything God ever wanted to do for you, He has already done. He declared it from the beginning. Isaiah 46:9-10 asserts: *"Remember the former things of old: for I am God, and there is none else, I am God, and there is none like me. Declaring the end from the beginning, and from ancient times the things that are not yet done, saying, My counsel shall stand, and I will do all my pleasure."*

God informs us that He declared the end from the beginning This illustrates to us that He has already completed you. He puts you back in time, then He starts you. It may seem strange but that is how God operates. He perfects his creation from the very beginning.

If we examine further the book of Revelation, Chapter 13, the latter part of verse 8 informs us that Jesus Christ existed even before the earth came to be *("...the lamb slain from the foundation of the world").* The lamb (Jesus) was sacrificed before there was a foundation. This is letting us know that God finishes us, then He start us. God has blessed us with all spiritual blessings in heavenly places in Christ Jesus. From the beginning of time, the Lamb, which is Jesus, was already slain before the foundation of the world. Hallelujah! The Creator refines and completes a product before He starts it. Man's tendency is to start a product, then try to finish it, but God works in the reverse.

We can rest in Him, because everything has been finished. Hebrews 4:3 states: *"For we which have believed do enter into rest, as he said, As I have sworn in my wrath, if they shall enter into my rest: although the works were finished from the foundation of the world."*

Chapter Three

Taking Authority by Speaking the Word Only

Take authority over your circumstances by speaking the word only. We know words are very powerful. Everything came into existence by the spoken word of God. Words are very powerful and can be used to change any circumstance. Matthew 8:8-10*: "The centurion answered and said, 'Lord, I am not worthy that thou shouldest come under my roof: but speak the word only, and my servant shall be healed. For I am a man under authority, having soldiers under me: and I say to this man, Go, and he goeth; and to another, Come, and he cometh: and to my servant, Do this, and he doeth it.' When Jesus heard it, he marveled, and said unto them that followed, 'verily I say unto you, I have not found so great faith, no, not in Israel.' "*

In order to be in authority, we must first come under authority. The centurion understood the power of words. He said to Jesus, 'Speak the word only and my servant shall be healed'. There was no doubt in his mind that if Jesus spoke, by his word, his servant would be healed. Words are very powerful especially when we speak with faith. When the word of God goes forth it will not return to us void. This means that it will not go out and be profitless, it will accomplish what God desires for it to accomplish. Since the Bible declares that, the angels of the Lord will hearken unto the voice of God's word, we must speak God's word in faith, knowing that what we have spoken will come to pass, it will be fulfilled.

Matthew 8:16 – ***"When the even was come, they brought unto him many that were possessed with devils: and he cast out the spirits with his***

36

word, and healed all that were sick." Even the devils are subjected to the word of God. Notice how He chased the spirits away. He spoke the word and the devils were cast out of the man. We too can speak God's word over any circumstance or situation, and it must change.

Words are sounds that have meaning. The universe will respond when we speak. When we speak a word, it goes out into the universe as a vibration, and whatever word we release, if it has been mixed with faith, it will not return void. It will do just what we commanded it to do.

John 6:63 reveals: *"It is the spirit that quickeneth; the flesh profits nothing: the words that I speak unto you, they are spirit, and they are life."* Jesus proclaims that the words that He speak are life. This means that the words are alive! When we speak, a spirit is attached to our words, giving life to whatever we say. Words can build someone up, or words can tear them down. Our words can lead to destruction. Jesus reminds us that the words that He speak are spirit, and they are life. When we speak, our purpose should be to encourage and uplift. Our words should intentionally give life.

The book of Hebrews, chapter 4 verse 12 indicates: ***"For the word of God is quick, and powerful, and sharper than any two edge sword, piercing even to the dividing asunder of soul and spirit, and of the joints and marrow, and is a discerner of the thoughts, and intents of the heart."*** The word of God is so powerful that it pierces the core of our soul. The word of God discerns our evil thoughts and the intentions of our hearts. When God speaks, the light that comes from His word causes the darkness to flee. Darkness cannot be in the presence of light: ***"Through faith,*** *we understand the worlds were framed by the word of God, so that things which are seen were not made of things which are visible"* (Hebrews 11:3).

Everything that exists came from the unseen world. God spoke the word and things came into existence. We are created in his image and in the likeness of God. We are speaking spirits, having an earthly experience. We also create our own reality by the words we speak. Everything that exists came forth by the spoken word. We must be very careful how we speak God's word. Isn't it amazing how we can speak a word and things react to it? Do you remember when Jesus came by the fig tree looking for figs and the tree did not produce any? The tree had leaves only. Seeing there was no fruit on the tree, he said, ***"Let no fruit grow on thee henceforward for ever,"*** and instantly the fig tree withered away. Jesus spoke to the fig tree and it responded*! "And when the disciples saw it, they marveled, saying, How soon is the fig tree withered away!"* (Matthew 21:18-22) The fig tree dried up from the root because of the spoken word.

Proverbs 18:21 lets us know, *"Death and life are in the power of the tongue: and they that love it shall eat the fruit thereof".* So, if life and death are in the power of your tongue, you chose, by your words, whether to live a happy life or a sad life. If you want good/positive, we must speak good/positive. Positive things come when we attract them in our lives. If we speak negatively, negative things will come. We attract to us what we speak and believe. We must stop saying, "I can't" and start saying "I can." The scriptures tell us 'we can do all things through Christ which strengtheneth us' (Philippians 4:13). There is no limit to what we can do.

Once, the disciples came to Jesus because they wanted to know why they could not cast out the devil as he had. ***"And Jesus said unto them, Because of your unbelief: for verily I say unto you, If ye have faith as a grain of mustard seed, ye shall say unto this mountain, Remove hence to yonder place; and it shall remove; and nothing shall be impossible unto you,"*** (Matthew 17:20). Jesus definitively explains that even a miniscule amount of faith can get the job done. We can speak the words, "Be removed," and it shall be removed. Nothing is impossible to those who believe. We can take authority over any situation by speaking the word. When spoken words are mixed with faith, they will not return void, but they will accomplish that which they were sent to do. Keep in mind that we are speaking spirits, having an earthly experience. The spirit was first, and then the natural man came after.

Taking authority over a dead situation must be practical. In the book of Ezekiel, chapter 37 beginning at verse one: ***"The hand of the Lord was upon me, and carried me out in the spirit of the Lord, and set me down in the midst of the valley which was full of bones."*** The spirit of the Lord took Ezekiel and put him in the midst of a situation in which everything was dead. In verse two he writes: ***"And caused me to pass by them round about: and, behold, there were very many in the open valley; and, lo they were very dry."*** Has God ever placed you in a situation where everything seems to be dry? Have you ever found yourself in a situation where everything seems to be dead?

The question is, why would God put someone in the midst of a situation where everything is dead? In verse three, God asked Ezekiel a question: *"And he said unto me, Son of man, can these bones live? And I answered, O Lord God, thou knowest."* In other words, Ezekiel replied, Lord you know whether or not these bones live. Sometimes, God will put us in a situation and ask us the question, 'Is there any hope for this situation? Can you bring this situation back to life?' Ezekiel examined the situation and came to the conclusion, 'Thou (God) knowest. He added in verse four: *"Again he said unto me, Prophesy upon these bones, and say unto them, O ye dry bones, hear the word of the Lord."* If we should elucidate this matter, what God wanted Ezekiel to do, was to speak over the dry bones and declare to them that they must hear and respond to the word of the Lord. The only way something dead can come to life is when we speak to it using God's authority, the Word. The word that Ezekiel prophesied spoke life into a dead situation. Ezekiel, acting in obedience, announces in verse five, *"Thus saith the Lord God unto these bones; Behold, I will cause breath to enter into you, and ye shall live."* In verse six, he writes, *"And I will lay sinews upon you, and will bring up flesh upon you, and cover you with skin, and put breath in you, and ye shall know that I am the Lord."*

It doesn't matter how big your situation may be. Your situation may look hopeless. Romans 4:17 teaches us that 'we can always call those things which be not as though they were.' We must therefore, come into agreement with our expected outcome even before we see it manifested in the physical realm. Even if you see no evidence of what you desire in sight, if you believe and declare that is so, then it will be.

In verse seven, Ezekiel states, ***"So I prophesy as I was commanded: and as I prophesied, there was a noise, and behold a shaking, and the bones came together, bone to his bone."*** Notice what happens when Ezekiel prophesied - there was a noise. Anytime you and I prophesy over a situation in our life that looks dead, we will always hear 'noise'. Noise is a distraction. Noise comes from the devil. He does not want you and I to speak God's word over our tumultuous situations. The first response to Ezekiel's prophecy was noise. Next, there was a shaking. A shaking indicates things are about to come together. Hallelujah! I said things are about to come together. The bones will scoot all over the valley. When the shaking stopped, bones came together, bone to his bone. Whenever something is out of order, you can always speak God's word and bring it back in line.

The noise and the shaking going on in the valley was an indicator that things were about to come together.

Continuing in verse eight, Ezekiel writes, *"And when I beheld, lo, the sinews and the flesh came up upon them, and the skin cover them above, but there was no breath in them."* The bones came together, but there was no life. Many churches today may be together, but they are lifeless, just as these dry bones in the valley. Without the word being activated, they are spiritually dead. Ezekiel was instructed to prophesy unto the wind. He prophesied, *"...Thus saith the Lord God; Come from the four winds, O breath, and breathe upon these slain, that they may live (verse nine)."* He prophesied as he was commanded and immediately breath came into the bones. They came to life and stood up on their feet

- an exceedingly great army. When we speak God's word over a dead situation, it is the spirit that gives our words life. The wind represents the Holy Spirit. Do you remember the miraculous events on the day of Pentecost, when the disciples were together in the upper room? They were all on 'one accord (meaning in agreement) and suddenly there came a sound from heaven like a mighty rushing wind and it filled the whole house'. They were seated and were all filled with the Holy Spirit. Even though things appear to be together, if there is no spirit, there is no life. It is the spirit that gives life!

Chapter Four

Taking Authority Over Your Minds

When we learn to take authority over our circumstances, we have actually learned to take authority over ourselves. Again, Jesus is the ultimate authority. His word is the final authority. When we stay connected to Jesus, there is nothing we cannot do. Scripture tells us we can do all things through Christ Jesus. Amen. Knowing who you are and whose you are is very important. If you do not know who you are, you will go through life not knowing your purpose. This book is designed to help you understand your God-given authority, and the legal rights we have on this Earth.

It is illegal for a spirit to operate in the earth realm without a body. We as human beings living

49

in a physical body have a legal right to operate in this realm. We were created and designed to inhabit planet Earth. We are speaking spirits having an earthly experience. When we speak, creation has to obey as though God has spoken. Everything God created came into existence by his spoken word. Words are very powerful. Words can also change your reality. Jesus said, ***"It is the spirit that quickeneth; the flesh profiteth nothing: the words that I speak unto you, they are spirit, and they are life (John 6:63)."***

Every word we speak has a spirit that is attached to it, so we must be careful how we use our words. When words and thoughts become one, they create our experience, and our experience becomes our reality. After reading this book, you will acquire the knowledge to govern your mind. Once you learn how to govern your thoughts, you can govern your words. We are a spirit living in a body and we possess a soul. Everything that exists today came from the spirit world. It was the spirit first, then the natural was later created.

What is your mind? Your mind is the part of you that processes thoughts. The mind consists of two parts: the conscious mind and the subconscious mind. The conscious mind includes such things as the sensation perception, memories, feelings and fantasies inside our current awareness. The subconscious mind is the part of consciousness that is not currently in focal (relating to the center or main point of interest) awareness. The subconscious mind is where we store memories; like a computer, it is where all habits are formed. We are what we think. Proverbs 23:7 reveals: ***"For as he thinketh in his heart, so is he."*** What he is really thinking about is himself. ***<u>The mind is the</u>***

51

**element of a person that enables he/she to be in a world of his/her own. He or she develops experiences to think and to feel the faculty of consciousness and thoughts.** Your mind is the place where you process thoughts. When we hold a thought long enough, it goes into the subconscious mind. We create our experiences by processing thoughts. You really can't trust your mind because your mind can fool you. Jesus made a powerful statement in Matthew 5:28 - _**"But I say unto you, That whosoever looketh on a woman to lust after her hath committed adultery with her already in his heart."**_ If you focus on something long enough, it will eventually get into your heart. When the mind and heart become one, your eye is acting as a singular component (one in agreement and harmony). Jesus further explicates this in Matthew 6:22-23: _**"The light of the body is the**_ *eye: if therefore thine eye be single; thy whole body shall be full of light. But if thy eye be evil, thy whole body shall be full of darkness. If therefore the light that is in thee be darkness, how great is that darkness!"*

What does Jesus mean when he says the body is the eye? He is talking about your spiritual eye. When your spiritual eye is open, then your whole life will irradiate like Christ. When your mind and heart become one you are now single-eyed. When your eye is single you are focused. When you are focused, you have complete control of your destiny. So, when Jesus said: 'if a man looks upon a woman to lust after her, in his heart he has already committed adultery', he is telling us we can sin in our heart without doing any physical act.

Our minds are very powerful. We must be aware of evil thoughts and learn to cast them down immediately. If you let a thought linger in your mind it will eventually get into your heart and the body will act it out. We must learn to control our minds. We must guard our minds by 'casting down all imaginations that try to exalt itself against the Word of God'. Keep in mind we create our own reality by what we believe to be true. What we believe to be the truth, may not be the truth, but our own perception.

Having the right mind can help us to manifest prosperity. God told Joshua, ***"This book of the law should not depart out of thy mouth; but thou shalt meditate therein day and night, that thou mayest observe to do according to all that is written therein: for then thou shalt make thy way prosperous, and then thou shalt have good success"*** (Joshua 1:8). When we meditate on God's Word, it gets into the subconscious mind becoming one with our hearts. The unity of our mind and heart gives us the ability to be prosperous, healthy and happy. The Word of God instructs us to think on these things: things that are 'true, honest, just, pure, lovely, and of good report'. It urges us to consider that if there is 'any virtue, and if there be any praise', that we should 'think on these things' (Phillipians 4:8). Positive thinking will attract positivity in your life. On the other hand, if you think about negative things, negativity will come to you.

Meditation is very powerful. Meditating or visualizing something gives you a clear picture of what you want. Meditating on the Word of God day and night allows the Word to get into your spirit. Once in your spirit, it begins to manifest through your actions. Romans 12:2 charges: ***And be not conformed to this world: but be ye***

55

transformed by the renewing of your mind, that ye may prove what is that good, and acceptable, and perfect, will of God." Through the transformation of our minds, we transform our lives. Meditating and focusing on the Word of God teaches us His perfect will.

The Apostle Paul instructs us, *"Let this mind be in you, which was also in Christ Jesus: Who, being in the form of God, thought it not robbery to be equal with God"* (Philippians 2:5-6). Christ has the mind of God, and we must have the mind of Christ. With the mind of Christ, we think like Christ, enabling us to do the things Christ did. Like Christ, we will see things through the eyes of God. When strongholds try to capture our minds, we can cast them down confidently knowing that, *'the weapons of our warfare are not carnal, but mighty through God to the pulling down of*

56

strongholds; casting down imaginations and every high thing that exalteth itself against the knowledge of God, and bringing into captivity every thought to the obedience of Christ" (2 Corinthians 10:4-5). We have this authority in Jesus' name.

Chapter Five

The Natural Man

"But the natural man receiveth not the things of the Spirit of God: for they are foolishness unto him: neither can he know them, because they are spiritually discerned" (1st Corinthians 2:14). Another translation of the Bible, The Contemporary English Version puts it this way: *"...only someone who has God's Spirit can understand spiritual blessings."* The natural man (mind) is not designed to recognize spiritual elements. However, through your spirit, you have discernment.

The natural man is the conscious, unspiritual mind. If you understood the things of God (that is, spiritual things) with your mind, then the natural man could understand them. But you don't. You discern them or understand them with your spirit. The natural man is the unspiritual physical man; his wisdom is earthly (earthly means natural). James describes it in the third chapter verses 14-15: ***"But if ye have bitter envying and strife in your hearts, glory not, and lie not against the truth. This wisdom descended not from above, but is earthly, sensual, devilish."***

The natural man is motivated by demons. He is ruled by Satan. I am not saying he is demon possessed. You see, all those who have never been born again have Satan as their God and father. They are in the kingdom of darkness and they are more or less ruled by Satan and his demons. As stated, the natural man cannot understand the things of the Spirit of God, they are foolishness to him. The Bible is the Spirit of God. It is not natural or human knowledge. Holy men of old wrote as they were moved by the Spirit of God; the Word of God is spiritually perceived.

We live in two worlds, the spiritual world and the physical world. Both worlds have laws and principles. Spiritual laws govern the spirit world, and the natural laws govern the physical world. We exist on earth in a physical body, but we are also seated in heavenly places in Christ Jesus: Ephesians 2:4-6 – ***"But God, who is rich in mercy, for His great love wherewith He loved us, Even when we were dead in sins, hath quickened us together with Christ (by grace ye are saved;) And hath raised us up together, and made us sit together in heavenly places in Christ Jesus"***.

When God created man, He gave him authority to operate in this earthly realm. A spirit cannot operate in the physical realm without a body. In order to operate in the spirit realm, we must use our spirit. We cannot do spiritual things with our natural mind. The physical realm consists of time, space and matter. In the garden of Eden, heaven and eternity was the atmosphere. Adam had a direct line to the Father. He communicated with the Father daily. But, when Adam sinned, he was temporarily disconnected from God. Whenever we sin it automatically disconnects us from the Spirit. When we are disconnected from the Spirit we can no longer communicate with the Father. Thank God for Jesus who came to reconnect us back to the Father.

Chapter Six

Taking Authority Over Self

The key to an abundant life is self-control. Self-control is the ability to direct one's emotions, behavior and desires in order to effectively function in society. If you cannot control yourself, it will be hard to control your destiny. We see this illustrated in Proverbs 25 verse 28: ***"He that hath no rule over his own spirit is like a city that is broken down, and without walls".***

People try to control others without first learning to control themselves. One of the ways we can control self, is by disciplining ourselves. Self-control is one of the fruits of the Spirit. The fruits of the Spirit are mentioned in Galatians 5:22-23: ***"But the fruit of the Spirit is love, joy, peace, long-suffering, gentleness, goodness, faith, meekness,*** *temperance (self-control) against such things there is no law."* If a man has self-control, it's a sign he has the spirit.

Paul writes in 2nd Timothy 1 verse 7: *"For God hath not given us the spirit of fear, but of power, and of love, and of a sound mind* (self-control)". When God created mankind, He gave us a sound mind. When self is in control, you will experience a battle of the mind. Those who belong to Christ Jesus learn to crucify passions and desires of the flesh. When we become born-again, our desires, should be His desires, our will should be His will.

Let's talk about what it means to crucify the flesh. The flesh is the part of us that resist our transformation into the new person that Christ Jesus has called us to be. The devil wants to use the pleasure of our flesh to keep us enslaved to old

64

habits and sinful attitudes. Remember what we said earlier, God did not give the natural man authority. He gave authority to the spirit man. Anytime we try to come up against the devil in our flesh; he will win every time because the natural man does not have authority. When we are in a spiritual battle, we must not rely on our own ability to win. We must rely on the Holy Spirit who is one congruence with our spirit.

By controlling our tongue, we control our destiny: James 3:7-8 – *"For every kind of beasts, and of birds, and of serpents, and of things in the sea, is tamed, and hath been tamed of mankind: But the tongue can no man tame; it is an unruly evil, full of deadly poison".* Our tongue, when it is guided by the ways of the natural man, is what gets us into trouble. This is why we need the Holy Spirit. The Holy Spirit will lead us and guide us in what to say. The Holy Spirit is also a keeper, comforter, and teacher. He is the one who knows the intentions of man's heart. This little tongue in our mouth is a very small but very powerful organ. James says, 'no man can tame it'. It is like a deadly poison very unruly and it is evil. If we can control our tongue, you will master self-control.

Chapter Seven

Taking Authority Over Our True Reality

Our true reality is not what we see, feel or touch. Our true reality is spiritual, because we are spiritual beings. We are taught in the gospel of Matthew, chapter 6 verse 10, that Jesus prayed, ***"Thy kingdom come. Thy will be done on earth, as it is in heaven".*** The will of the Father is for earth to be like heaven. We are in this physical world, but in reality, we are seated in heavenly places in Christ Jesus. We are here on Earth, but we are also there, in Heaven. This is seen in Ephesians chapter 2, verses 5-6: ***"Even when we were dead in sins, hath quickened us together with Christ, (by grace ye are saved;) And hath raised us up together, and made us sit together in heavenly places in Christ Jesus".*** God has already

67

given us authority over here (earth) and there (heaven).

In our reality, we have keys. For example, Jesus said in Matthew 16:19: ***"And I will give unto thee the keys of the kingdom of heaven: and whatsoever thou shalt bind on earth shall be bound in heaven: and whatsoever thou shalt loose on earth, shall be loosed in heaven."*** There are seven principles of keys. Once we know the principles behind keys, we can understand how they work in the kingdom. Keys represent --

- **authority** and **access**: A key gives you instant access to everything.

- **ownership** and **control**: If you possess the key to something, you can control it.

- **authorization**: When you are given a key, you are being authorized to act in the name (or in the stead) of the one who gave you the keys.

- **<u>power</u>**: Whoever gives you keys, empower you at the same time.

- **<u>freedom</u>**: When you have keys, you are free to go in and out. You have the authority to lock and unlock.

The question is, how do you get access to these keys? Jesus said to Peter (Matthew 16:18*): "And I say also unto thee, That thou art Peter, upon this rock I will build my church; and the gates of hell shall not prevail against it. And I will give unto thee the keys of the kingdom of heaven: and whatsoever thou shalt bind on earth shall be bound in heaven: and whatsoever thou shall loose on earth shall be loosed in heaven".*

Jesus is actually saying to Peter, because my father has revealed unto you who I am, now, you have the keys to the kingdom. You have access to everything in the kingdom of God, and God will back you up. Whatever you loose (release or

69

detach) on earth, will be loosed (released or detached) in heaven. When we become born again, filled with His Holy Spirit, we gain access to the kingdom of God. This is evident in Paul's gospel of Ephesians, chapter 1 verse 3: "Blessed be the God and Father of our Lord Jesus Christ, who hath blessed us with all spiritual blessings in heavenly places in Christ."

My brothers and sisters, God has already blessed us with all spiritual blessings even before the foundation of the world. We can use our faith to go into the spirit realm and bring our blessings to our now - our present reality. When we learn how to give our faith an assignment, faith will work for us every time. Many people today are trying to believe God for something that they already have. God has blessed all of us with all spiritual blessings. We need to give our faith an assignment.

We walk by faith and not by sight. You cannot believe everything you see, because what you see may not be true. It is only our perception.

Your mind can fool you. The Scripture says ***"Let this mind be in you, which was also in Christ Jesus"*** (Philippians 2:5). We need the mind of Christ in order to see things the way Christ sees things. When we have the mind of Christ, we can see things through the spiritual lens and mind of Christ. When we rely on our own minds and abilities, we are subject to failure.

An in-depth look at Mark chapter 11 verse 22 speaks about Christ-like faith: ***"And Jesus answering saith unto them, Have faith in God."*** The writer is imploring us to have the God kind of faith. Jesus uses these precepts to teach his disciples that they must know that 'all things are possible to them that believe'. When we have the

God kind of faith we can speak to mountains and/or any situation in our lives. Using our key of authority in the spoken Word, we can say to circumstances be removed and our circumstances will be removed. This is reiterated in verse 23 of Mark 11, Jesus said, *"For verily I say unto you, That whosoever shall say unto this mountain, Be thou removed, and be thou cast into the sea; and shall not doubt in his heart, but shall believe that those things which he saith shall come to pass; he shall have whatsoever he saith".*

If you believe what you say will come to pass, it will happen. Praise the Lord! One thing that keeps us in bondage is exposed: UNBELIEF. If you don't believe your words are valuable, what good are your words? Verse 24 adds: *"Therefore I say unto you, What things soever ye desire, when ye pray, believe that ye receive them, and ye shall have them"*. Jesus is saying we must believe before we receive. How can we believe before we actually receive? Well, first we must see it in our minds. Next, we have to act as though we have already received it, and then, we shall have it. Many people want to believe something after they receive. But the Father wants us to believe before we actually receive. This is called faith. Faith is believing something without actually seeing it or touching it with our physical body*: "Now faith is the substance of things hoped for, the evidence of things not seen"* (Hebrews 11:1). The Bible lets us know, *"But without faith it is impossible to please him (God): for he that cometh to God must believe that he is, and that he is a rewarder of them that diligently seek him"* (Hebrews 11:6).

Chapter Eight

Taking Authority Over the Spirit of Bondage

The Spirit of bondage can be brought about when an individual is possessed, oppressed or in rebellion against God; submitting to the sins of the flesh. Millions of people are in bondage or oppressed by the spirit of bondage. The Bible makes it very clear, there are demons, or evil spirits in the world that interfere in our lives. Ephesians 6:11-12 instructs us: ***"Put on the whole armor of God, that ye may be able to stand against the wiles of the devil. For we wrestle not against flesh and blood, but against principalities, against powers, against the rulers of the darkness of this world, against spiritual wickedness in high places."*** Our fight is not against one another but against the powers, principalities (satan and his demons) and

75

rulers (political leaders) of this world. They are the ones in high places (government) who rage wars against our spirit man.

The only way we can fight against the wiles of the devil, is to equip ourselves by putting on the whole armor of God. It is hard to fight an enemy you cannot see. The devil wants us to think he does not exist. There is a real devil and his objective is to destroy the plans and people of God. The devil does not want us to know he is already defeated. He also does not want us to know the authority we have in the name of Jesus. There is power in the name of Jesus. I must reiterate this point: there is power in the name of Jesus! This is echoed in the book of Philippians, chapter 2, verses 10 to 11: *"That at the name of Jesus every knee should bow, of things in heaven, and things on earth, and things under the earth; And that every tongue should confess that Jesus Christ is Lord, to the glory of God the Father."* Satan must and will bow! Hallelujah!

Our battle is not with one another but against principalities. Ephesians 6:13 puts it rightly: *"Wherefore take unto you the whole armor of God, that ye may be able to withstand in the evil day, and having done all, to stand."* When you have done all you can do, the Apostle Paul says just stand. There will be some evil days ahead. However, when we put on the whole armor of God, what the devil tries to do against us, will not work: *'...when the enemy shall come in like a flood, the Spirit of the Lord shall lift up a standard against him* (Isaiah 59:19)'.

Ephesians 6:14 invites us to *"Stand therefore, having your loins girt about with truth, and having on the breastplate of righteousness."*

When we put on the 'breastplate of righteousness', the enemy cannot penetrate our hearts. The 'breastplate of righteousness', means our heart is covered. Whenever your heart is covered, nothing and nobody can hurt you.

The breastplate of goodness protects you. When you know your heart and motives are right, you will not be convicted by the accusations of the enemy. In a spiritual battle, we must not forget to 'stand having our loins girt about with truth', and our 'feet shod with the preparation of the gospel of peace'. When facing a spiritual battle, know this, God has already given you everything you need to endure and conquer. The devil has already been defeated. Jesus defeated him over 2000 years ago when he was nailed to the cross. The devil knows he is defeated, and he does not want us to know. If we know that he is not a real threat, he loses his

78

influence.

In Ephesians 6:16, Paul bids us to arm ourselves so that we may be able to effectively conquer the enemy: *"Above all, take the shield of faith, wherewith ye shall be able to quench all the fiery darts of the wicked."* As mentioned earlier, the devil needs a body or a person to work through. Don't take it personal when someone comes to you, trying to bring confusion, negative ideas or thoughts. It's a sign that they are being influenced by an evil spirit. Don't look at the person. Look into their heart to understand who is behind the scene.

As is declared in Ephesians 6:17, *"We must also take the helmet of salvation, and the sword of the spirit, which is the word of God."* The helmet of salvation is protection for our minds. Every soldier going into battle must put on a helmet.

Notice, there is only one weapon mentioned - the sword of the Spirit, which is the Word of God. All we need when we are in a spiritual battle is the Word of God. God's Word is *'...quick, powerful, and sharper than any two-edged sword'* (Hebrews 4:12). 'When the enemy comes in like a flood', the Word of God will cut him down every time. When we speak truth, it pierces the heart of our enemy. Truth liberates, setting those in bondage free. Never go into battle without putting on the whole armor of God.

I would have already mentioned that it is illegal for a spirit to operate in the earth realm without a body. The devil knows he is out of order and in need of a body to operate in the earth realm (which was created for human habitation). He used (possessed) the serpent in the Garden of Eden so he could beguile Eve. His tactics have not changed.

He uses (temporarily possessing) people to work against one another. The Word of truth lets us know our battle is not with one another, but against the evil forces of darkness.

Spiritual bondage can keep a person in a state of depression and causes physical harm to the body. The Bible makes it clear: ***"The thief cometh not, but for to steal, and to kill, and to destroy: Jesus said, I come that they might have life, and that they might have it more abundantly"*** (John 10:10). The devil's goal is to steal your health; steal your relationships with family; steal finances, and prematurely take lives. Jesus came that we may have abundant and full lives. The Father's desire and heart is for us to live a life full of his blessings.

The next time you feel the spirit of depression or a spirit of bondage trying to come into your life, speak the Word. Every spirit is subject to and must obey the Word of the Lord. Always be mindful and make it a practice to meditate on 2nd Timothy chapter 1, verse 7: **"For God hath not given us a spirit of fear; but of power, and of love, and of a sound mind."** When God sets us free, we are free indeed! The only thing that can keep us in bondage, is self. Self is our greatest enemy. When we learn how to take authority over self, the devil won't have anything to work with.

1st John 4:1-2 admonishes us: *"Beloved, believe not every spirit, but try the spirits, whether they are of God: because many false prophets are gone out into the world".* Hereby know ye the spirit of God: Every spirit that confesses that Jesus Christ is come in the flesh is of God". Scripture tells us not to believe every spirit, because the devil's job is to deceive us. He is inclined to keep us confused and doubtful concerning Jesus. We can try the spirit by the Spirit, if we have the Spirit of God. In order to <u>take authority,</u> we must be fully empowered by the Spirit of God. Becoming one with the Father, through belief and acceptance of the redemptive work of His Son, Jesus, places us in right standing with God. He therefore equips us with His Spirit, giving us the keys to His kingdom (and kingdom concepts).

Chapter Nine

Take Authority Over Your Garden

God has given us charge over all He created. We have the responsibility of taking care of our own garden. When God created Adam, He placed him in the Garden of Eden giving him instructions to dress and keep it. Adam was responsible for whatever happened in the garden: *"And the Lord God commanded the man, saying of every tree of the garden thou mayest freely eat: But of the tree of the knowledge of good and evil, thou shalt not eat of it: for in the day that thou eatest thereof thou shalt surely die"* (Genesis 2:16-17).

After God gave Adam instructions, He brought his wife, Eve to him. This is seen in Genesis 2:18*: "And the Lord God said, It is not good that the man should be alone; I will make*

85

him a help meet for him". God gave the man (Adam) instructions and vision for his family before He presented his wife. A man must be ready, with a vision for his family before he commits to taking a wife. A man with no vision for his family will always frustrate his wife because she is a helper; designed to help him meet his responsibilities towards God.

One day when Eve was in the garden, the serpent had a conversation with her. He was intriguing and influencing her to question God's instructions concerning the tree of the knowledge of good and evil: Genesis 3:1: *"And he said unto the woman, Yea, hath God said, Ye shall not eat of every tree of the garden?"* After Eve repeated God's instructions in error, the serpent replied, *"Ye shall not surely die: For God doth know that in the day ye eat thereof, then your eyes shall be opened, and ye shall be as gods, knowing good and evil. And when Eve saw that the tree was good for food, and that it was pleasant to the eyes, and a tree to be desired to make one wise, she took of the fruit thereof, and did eat, and gave also unto her husband with her; and he did eat."* (Genesis 3:4-6) On this day, Adam did not take authority. He allowed the enemy to come into his garden, which ultimately caused a separation between him and his God.

The question frequently asked is - 'Why didn't God stop him?' We create our experiences according to what we believe to be true. God has given every man free-will to choose life or death. Adam chose death because he wanted to experience the difference between life and death. Disobedience always brings with it, a type of death. Thoughts and emotions becoming one (unified) give rise to feelings. Feelings come from you like a vibration, attracting to you what you feel to be truth and what you choose to experience. Adam attracted death to himself. It all starts in the subconscious mind. Your subconscious mind is like a computer storing memories and habits. All learned behaviors are in the subconscious mind. Proverbs 18:21 reminds us that ***"Death and life are in the power of the tongue: and they that love it shall eat the fruit thereof."*** Adam could have taken authority over his circumstances, just by speaking the word NO.

We can create our own experience by taking authority of what we say. If you say I am not going to make it, then most likely you will not make it. Many people look to others to help them navigate through life. But at the end of the day, it still boils down to what you believe to be the truth, and what you will accept. Our garden is our sacred place, and we should never let anyone, or anything disrupt it. The wise who understands this, seek to use the right words: words that correct, heal, restore, strengthen and tear down strongholds around them. People who do not understand this principle thoughtlessly create injury and chaos by the negative things they say, accept and expect. Words are very powerful; words create our experiences. We use words to take authority over our enemies. As referenced earlier, Ephesians 6:12 asserts: ***"For we wrestle not against flesh and blood, but against principalities, against powers, against the rulers of the darkness of this world, against spiritual wickedness in high places"***.

I John 4:4 further highlights***: "Ye are of God, little children, and have overcome them: because greater is he that is in you than he that is in the***

89

world." This greatness in you is the Holy Spirit. He is the one that keeps and guides you into your destiny. He helps us make the right decision when we do not know what to do. In every crisis area of life, He shows us exactly what to do. On the inside of you is a power giving you the ability to illuminate your mind and make the right decisions.

Become acquainted with the Holy Spirit, who will lead and guide you into all truth, and manifest Himself unto you. Isn't it amazing that if we do the same things repeatedly, we will get the same results? If we want to change anything, the change must first begin in us. We are creatures of habit, and we do not like change. Change can be good, especially changes for the better. Change also creates new experiences for those who are not afraid of change. When change comes, it brings fresh ideas, and fresh thoughts. Ideas help you create your own experiences. Adam wanted a different experience, so he submitted to the thought of eating from the tree of knowledge of good and evil. The end result, he opened the door to experiencing the unknown, death.

There was a time in my life when I wanted something better. I was working hard doing construction work, but all the time I was thinking, there has to be a better way. As I acknowledged this thought and began meditating on it, the idea came to my mind to start my own business. I began to write down (not only on paper but in my heart also) my thoughts and ideas. Emerging thoughts and ideas together formed a mental picture in my mind, and I knew starting my own business could become a reality, and it did. My thoughts became an idea, my idea became a mental picture in my mind, and then it became a reality.

If you can visualize what you want in life, or how you want your life to be, it can become your life experience. You have the authority to change any circumstance in your garden. Remember what I said in the previous chapters, when thoughts and emotions become one, they produce feelings. Feelings come from you like a vibration. This vibration operates in the atmosphere, attracting you to what you choose to experience. Your vibrations are like radio signals. You will attract and connect to signals based on your frequency. If you think on positive things, you are on a high frequency. If you are thinking negatively, you are on a low frequency. Start thinking about things that are pure, just, of good report, and good things will find you. Be at peace with yourself and let the Holy Spirit guide your life every day. Whoever is in charge of your life will be the one that dominate and control your destiny. If you are in charge, you are the one sitting on the throne of your life. If the Holy Spirit is sitting on the throne, then He is in charge. If we take a backseat and let the Holy Spirit take control, He will bring us to an expected end.

Life is like a game. We win some and we lose some. The important aspect of life is understanding how to play the game. Life will give you exactly what you put into it. Everything we do in life reflects back on us. Can I show you how life works? *"Be not deceived; God is not mocked: for whatsoever a man soweth that shall he also reap. For he that soweth to the flesh shall of the flesh reap corruption; but he that soweth unto the Spirit, shall of the Spirit reap life everlasting"* (Galatians 6:7-8). Life is about sowing and reaping, so get in the game and start sowing good seeds. You will be amazed at the harvest.

Chapter Ten

Only Believe

Believe means to accept something as truth, to feel sure of the truth. Jesus stated, *'all things are possible, to them that believe'.* When thoughts become one with your heart, it becomes your belief. Belief produces emotions, emotions produce feelings, feelings will produce your experience, and experiences create your current reality. When we take authority over our circumstances, we must believe what we say to be the truth. Many people today do not believe what they say can become true.

Matthew 21:19-21 states, *"And when he saw a fig tree in the way, he came to it, and found nothing thereon, but leaves only, and said unto it, Let no fruit grow on thee henceforward forever.*

95

And presently the fig tree withered away. When the disciples saw it, they marveled, saying, How soon is the fig tree withered away! Jesus answered and said unto them, Verily I say unto you, if ye have faith, and doubt not, ye shall not only do this which is done to the fig tree, but also if you shall say unto this mountain, Be thou remove, and be thou cast into the sea; it shall be done".

The key word is doubt. When someone doubts, they are saying, I really don't believe. Notice what Jesus said to his disciples, *'if ye have faith, you can speak to your mountains,* (or any situation, that is hindering you from going forth in life*), be thou removed it shall be done.'* There is power in words! We can speak to any situation with faith, and our words will not return void, because they are mixed with faith. All things are

96

possible to those who believe! So, we can move mountains with our words and our faith. Nothing is impossible to those who believe.

Jesus displayed authority that was given by God the Father: ***"And when Jesus came into the temple, the chief priests and the elders of the people came unto him as he was teaching, and said, By what authority doest thou these things? And who gave thee this authority?"*** (Matthew 21:23) They were hoping to trap him. If he claimed to have authority in himself as the son of God, they would accuse him of blasphemy. If he claimed authority from men, they would discredit him. If he claimed having authority from God, they would challenge him. No matter what Jesus did, they always try to find fault. Likewise, it doesn't matter what we try to do in life there will always be someone trying to find fault or stop us from moving forward. We must learn to take our God given authority and move in life without reservation. If we don't, or if we stop believing in ourselves, we will always go through life wondering what is true. Jesus said, *"And ye shall know the truth, and the truth shall set you free"* (John 8:32); free from self, free from lies, free from condemnation, and free from false accusations. When we align our spirits to the Spirit of God, we will know the truth.

There is a difference between truth and a fact. A fact can be changed, but the truth will never change. It is the truth that can change a fact. When we stand for that which is true, the Holy Spirit will stand with us. Do not allow doubt in your heart, only believe. The Holy Spirit will guide you to truth and will teach you the things of God. The Lord said unto Joshua, *"This book of the law shall not depart out of thy mouth; but thou shalt*

98

meditate therein day and night, that thou mayest observe to do according to all that is written therein: for then thou shalt make thy way prosperous, and then thou shalt have good success" (Joshua 1:8). The Holy Spirit will only bring to you what you have already studied in God's Word. When we meditate on the Word of God day in and day out it gets into our spirit. Scripture tells us, faith cometh by hearing, and hearing by the Word of God (2 Corinthians 5:17). When trouble comes, the Holy Spirit will bring back to our remembrance the Word we have studied, enabling us to speak the Word over our circumstances.

In my conclusion, let me remind you, God has given us all, authority over our circumstances, and free will to choose. Whenever we make a decision about a situation, we must remember there will always be consequences. There is always a reaction to every action; you are always presented with choices, and you must choose. No one can choose for you. The Father places life and death before us. If we choose life, life will be yours for the taking. If you choose death, you will no longer have life: "Beloved, I wish above all things that thou mayest prosper and be in health, even as thy soul prospereth" (3 John 1:2). A similar sentiment is repeated in verse 11: *"Beloved, follow not that which is evil, but that which is good. He that doeth good is of God: but he that doeth evil hath not seen God."*

It is your choice, **CHOOSE LIFE!!**

About the Author

Ronnie L. McCray and his wife reside in Cary, NC. They are the blessed parents of six children, eight grandchildren and a spiritual daughter. A native of South Carolina, his parents are Pastor Ronnie & Mary Lee McCray. Raised in the church it was evident he was called to ministry. At the age of five his father made him a green robe, he began preaching, and laying hands on people praying for their healing. His high school friends remember him preaching to them as he drove the school bus.

Dr. McCray was ordained at the age of 24, shortly after installed as pastor and has faithfully served in this capacity over 34 years. The foundation of his ministry is faith. Consistently teaching faith, one day the Father told him he would learn to live by faith. His faith journey has equipped him to understand and demonstrate Taking Authority Over Your Circumstances.

www.ingramcontent.com/pod-product-compliance
Lightning Source LLC
Chambersburg PA
CBHW060807110426
42739CB00032BA/3134